PIANO · VOCAL · GUITAR

THE BEST BROADWAY SONGS EVER

5TH EDITION

P9-CFM-366

ISBN 978-0-7935-0628-6

HAL•LEONARD®
CORPORATION

7777 W. BLUEMOUND RD. P.O. BOX 13819 MILWAUKEE, WI 53213

Visit Hal Leonard Online at
www.halleonard.com

CONTENTS
THE BEST BROADWAY SONGS EVER - 5TH EDITION

ALL GOOD GIFTS
from the Musical GODSPELL

Music by STEPHEN SCHWARTZ
Lyrics by MATTHIAS CLAUDIUS (1782)
Translated by JANE M. CAMPBELL (1861)

We plow the fields _ and scat - ter _ The
thank Thee, then _ O Fa - ther, For

good seed on _ the land, But it is fed _ and
all things bright _ and good, The seed time and _ the

ALL I ASK OF YOU
from THE PHANTOM OF THE OPERA

Music by ANDREW LLOYD WEBBER
Lyrics by CHARLES HART
Additional Lyrics by RICHARD STILGOE

No more talk of dark - ness, for - get these wide - eyed fears: I'm

here, noth - ing can harm you, my words will warm and calm you.

Let me be your free - dom, let day - light dry your tears: I'm

13

ALL THE THINGS YOU ARE

from VERY WARM FOR MAY

Lyrics by OSCAR HAMMERSTEIN II
Music by JEROME KERN

AS LONG AS HE NEEDS ME

from the Broadway Musical OLIVER!

Words and Music by
LIONEL BART

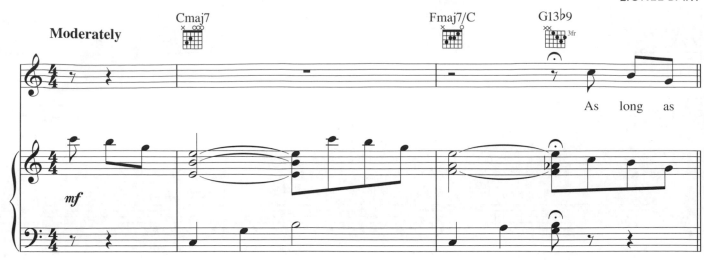

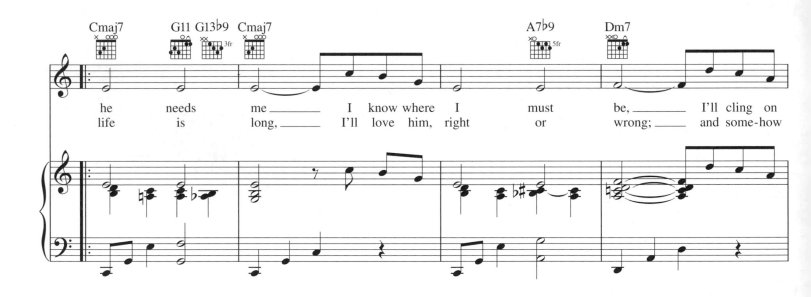

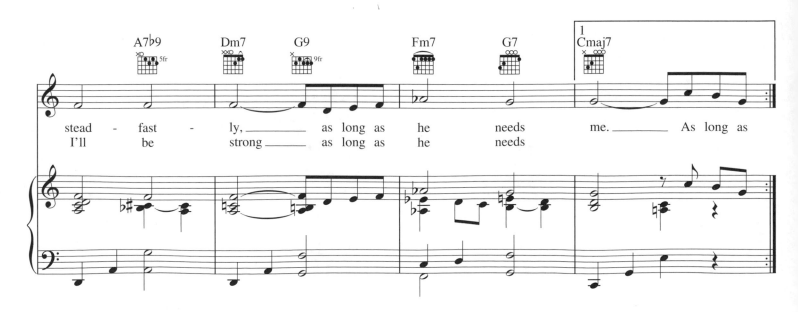

BEING ALIVE

from COMPANY

Words and Music by
STEPHEN SONDHEIM

CLIMB EV'RY MOUNTAIN

from THE SOUND OF MUSIC

Lyrics by OSCAR HAMMERSTEIN II
Music by RICHARD RODGERS

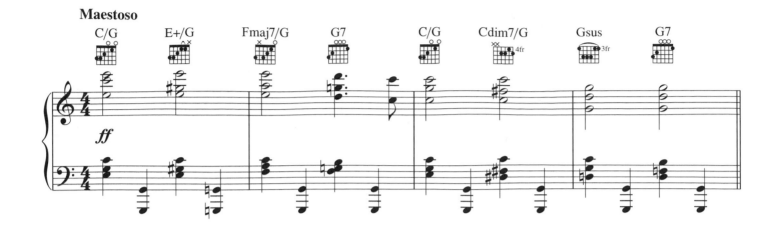

Climb ev - 'ry moun - tain, search high and low,

Fol - low ev - 'ry by - way, ev - 'ry path you know.

BEWITCHED
from PAL JOEY

Words by LORENZ HART
Music by RICHARD RODGERS

* *Standard lyric (in italics)*
** *Original show lyric.*

Lately I've not slept a wink, Since this half - pint im - i - ta - tion
I've done pret - ty well, I think, But this half - pint im - i - ta - tion

Put me on the blink. I'm wild a - gain, Be -
Put me on the blink. I'm wild a - gain! Be -
Seen a lot; I
Sweet a - gain, Pe -

guiled a - gain, A sim - per - ing, whim - per - ing child a - gain. Be -
guiled a - gain! A sim - per - ing, whim - per - ing child a - gain. Be -
mean a lot! But now I'm like sweet sev - en - teen a lot. Be -
tite a - gain, And on my pro - ver - bi - al seat a - gain. Be -

witched, both - ered and be - wil - dered am I.
witched, both - ered and be - wil - dered am I.
witched, both - ered and be - wil - dered am I.
witched, both - ered and be - wil - dered am I.

BRING HIM HOME

from LES MISÉRABLES

Music by CLAUDE-MICHEL SCHÖNBERG
Lyrics by HERBERT KRETZMER and ALAIN BOUBLIL

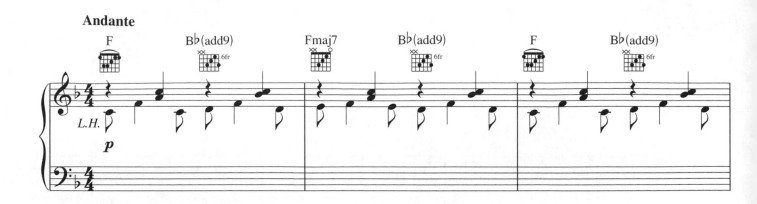

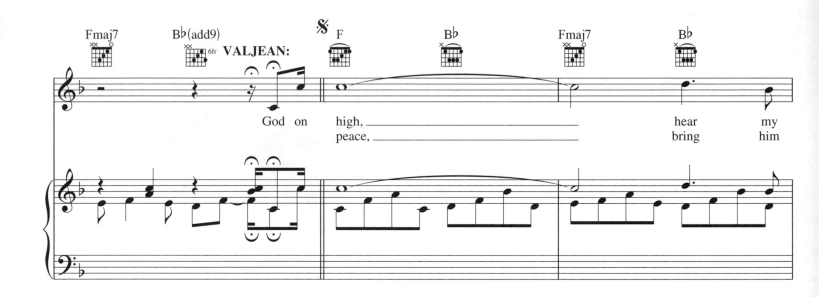

CABARET
from the Musical CABARET

Words by FRED EBB
Music by JOHN KANDER

CAMELOT
from CAMELOT

Words by ALAN JAY LERNER
Music by FREDERICK LOEWE

DON'T CRY FOR ME ARGENTINA

from EVITA

Words by TIM RICE
Music by ANDREW LLOYD WEBBER

look at me to know that ev - 'ry word is true.

FALLING IN LOVE WITH LOVE

from THE BOYS FROM SYRACUSE

Words by LORENZ HART
Music by RICHARD RODGERS

FORTY-SECOND STREET
from 42ND STREET

Words by AL DUBIN
Music by HARRY WARREN

GETTING TO KNOW YOU

from THE KING AND I

Lyrics by OSCAR HAMMERSTEIN II
Music by RICHARD RODGERS

It's a ver-y an-cient say-ing But a true and hon-est thought, That if you be-come a teach-er, by your pu-pils you'll be taught. As a teach-er, I've been

GOOD MORNING BALTIMORE

from HAIRSPRAY

Music by MARC SHAIMAN
Lyrics by MARC SHAIMAN and SCOTT WITTMAN

fan - ta - sy. Ev - 'ry sound's like a sym - pho - ny.
bar - room stool. They wish me luck on my way to school.

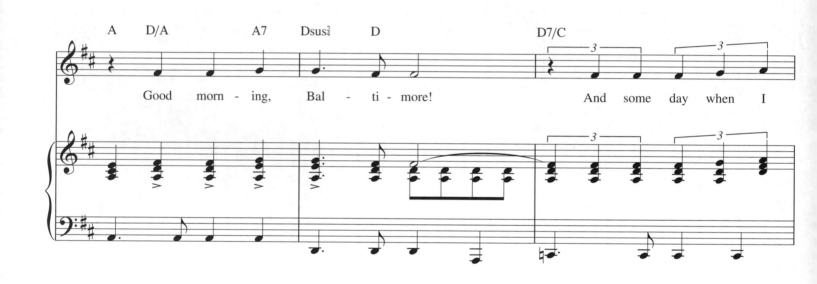

Good morn - ing, Bal - ti - more! And some day when I

take to the floor, the world's gon - na wake up and __ see

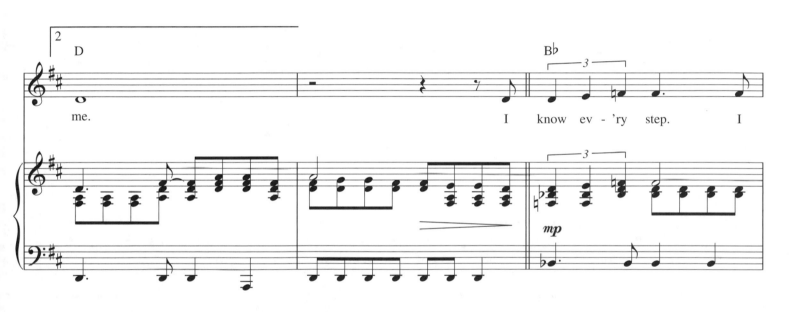

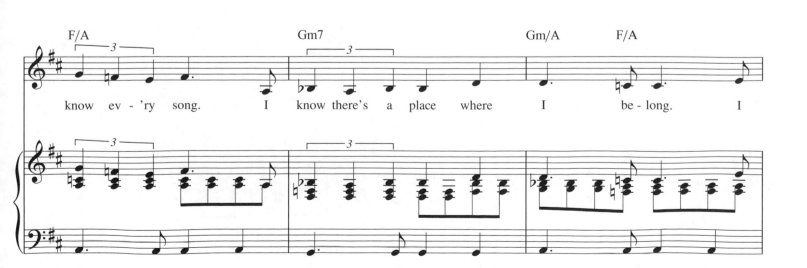

GOOD MORNING STARSHINE

from the Broadway Musical Producion HAIR

Words by JAMES RADO and GEROME RAGNI
Music by GALT MacDERMOT

HELLO, DOLLY!

from HELLO, DOLLY!

Music and Lyric by
JERRY HERMAN

Medium Strut

Hel - lo, Dol - ly, well, hel - lo, Dol - ly, it's so nice to have you back where you be - long. You're look - ing swell, Dol - ly, we can tell,

84

HEY THERE

from THE PAJAMA GAME

Words and Music by RICHARD ADLER
and JERRY ROSS

Hey there, _____ you with the stars in your eyes,

love nev-er made a fool of you, You used to be too wise! _____

_____ Hey there, _____ you on that high fly-ing

HELLO, YOUNG LOVERS

from THE KING AND I

Lyrics by OSCAR HAMMERSTEIN II
Music by RICHARD RODGERS

HOW ARE THINGS IN GLOCCA MORRA

from FINIAN'S RAINBOW

Words by E.Y. "YIP" HARBURG
Music by BURTON LANE

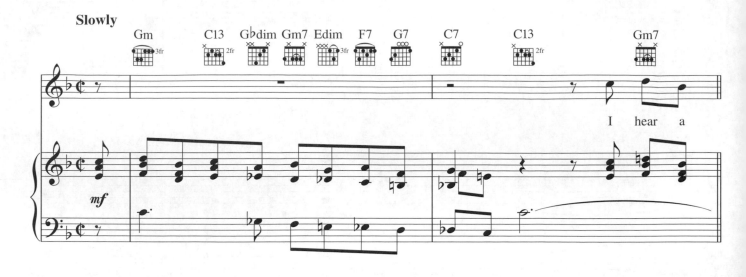

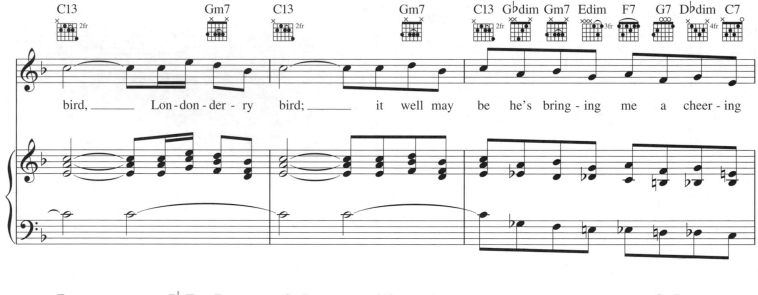

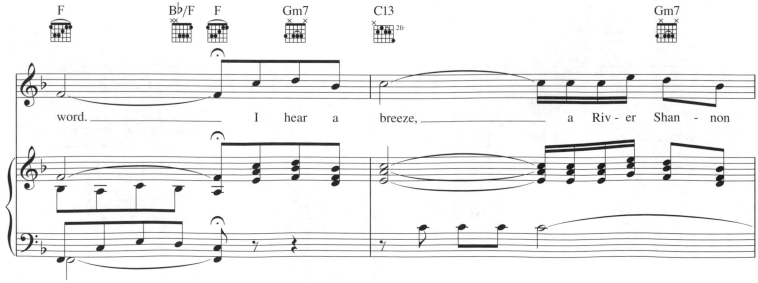

I BELIEVE IN YOU
from HOW TO SUCCEED IN BUSINESS WITHOUT REALLY TRYING

By FRANK LOESSER

I COULD HAVE DANCED ALL NIGHT

from MY FAIR LADY

Words by ALAN JAY LERNER
Music by FREDERICK LOEWE

I WANNA BE A PRODUCER

from THE PRODUCERS

Music and Lyrics by
MEL BROOKS

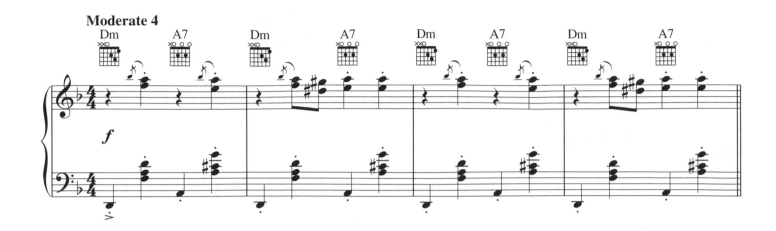

LEO & ACCOUNTANTS:

Un - hap - py, un - hap - py, ver - - - y un - hap - py,

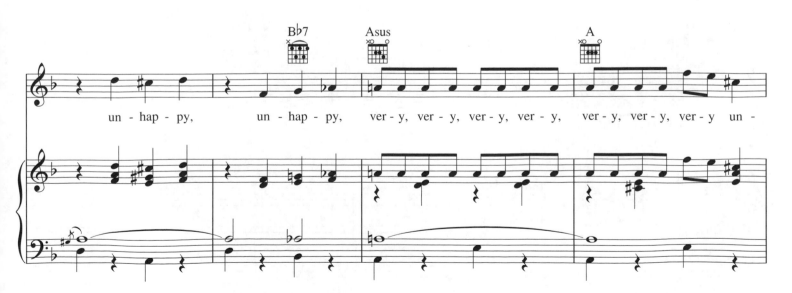

un - hap - py, un - hap - py, ver - y, ver - y, ver - y, ver - y, ver - y, ver - y, ver - y un -

SOLO ACCOUNTANT:

hap - py. Oh, I deb - its all de morn - in' and I

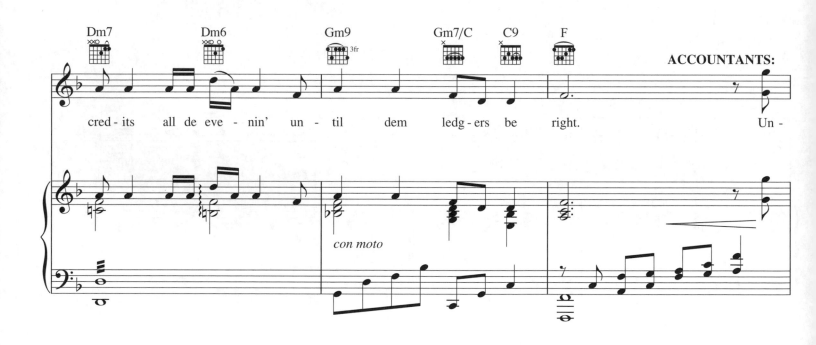

ACCOUNTANTS:

cred - its all de eve - nin' un - til dem ledg - ers be right. Un -

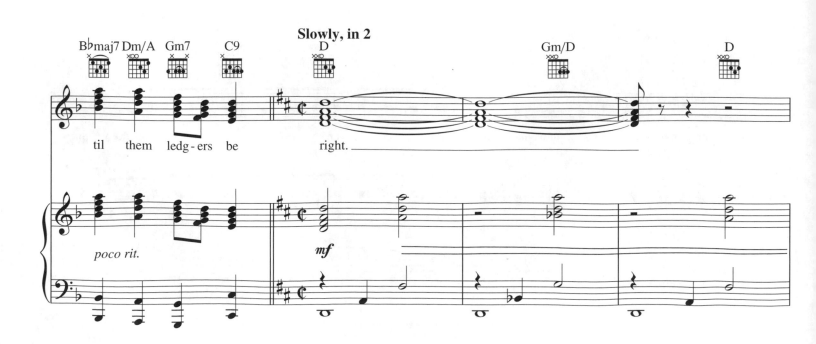

til them ledg - ers be right. _____

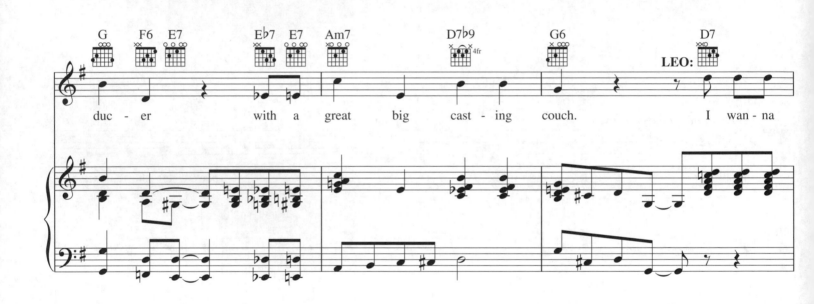

I DON'T KNOW HOW TO LOVE HIM

from JESUS CHRIST SUPERSTAR

Words by TIM RICE
Music by ANDREW LLOYD WEBBER

I DREAMED A DREAM

from LES MISÉRABLES

Music by CLAUDE-MICHEL SCHÖNBERG
Lyrics by ALAIN BOUBLIL, JEAN-MARC NATEL
and HERBERT KRETZMER

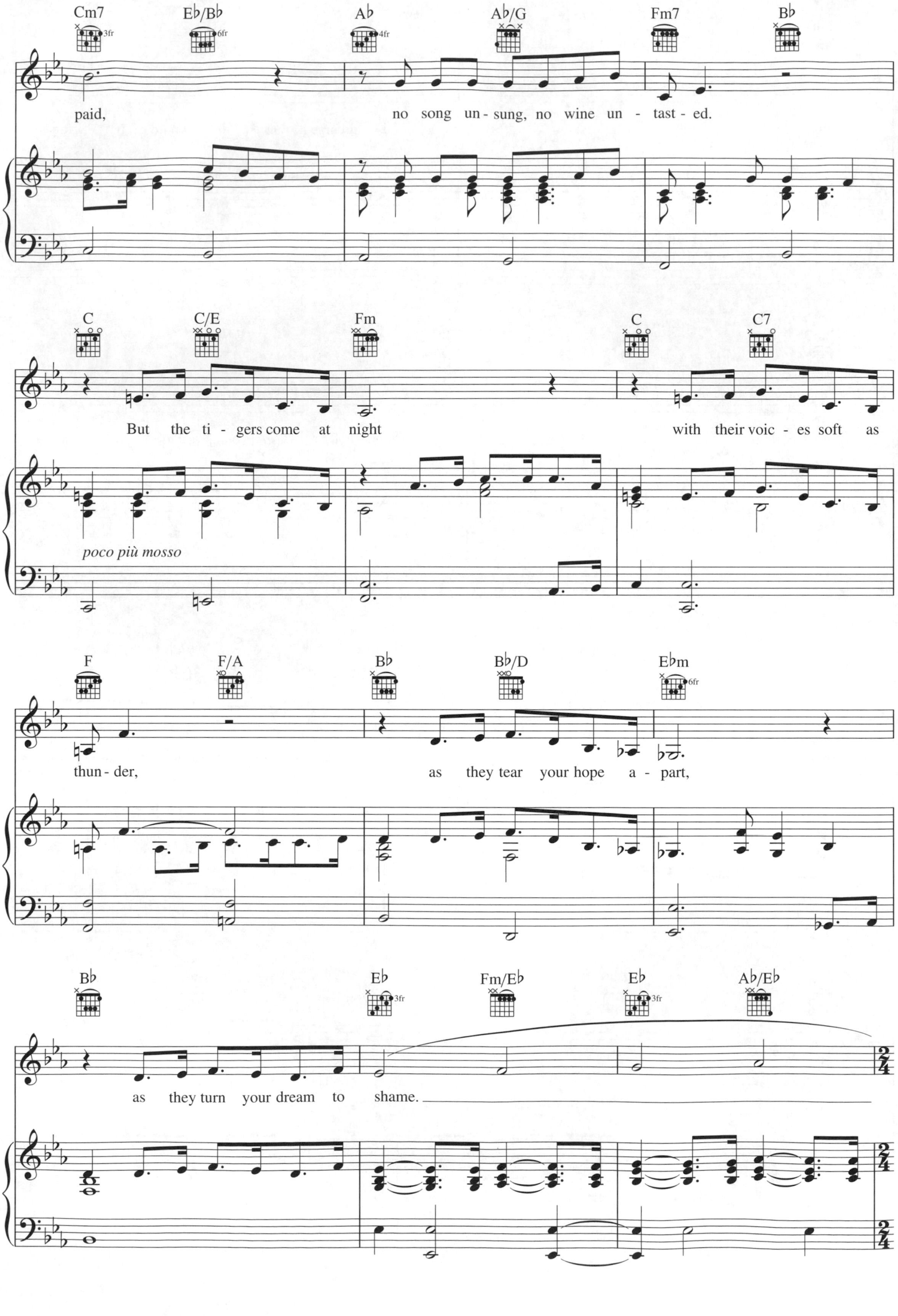

Cm7 E♭/B♭ A♭ A♭/G Fm7 B♭
paid, no song un - sung, no wine un - tast - ed.
C C/E Fm C C7
But the ti - gers come at night with their voic - es soft as
poco più mosso
F F/A B♭ B♭/D E♭m
thun - der, as they tear your hope a - part,
B♭ E♭ Fm/E♭ E♭ A♭/E♭
as they turn your dream to shame.

I GOT RHYTHM

from GIRL CRAZY

Music and Lyrics by GEORGE GERSHWIN
and IRA GERSHWIN

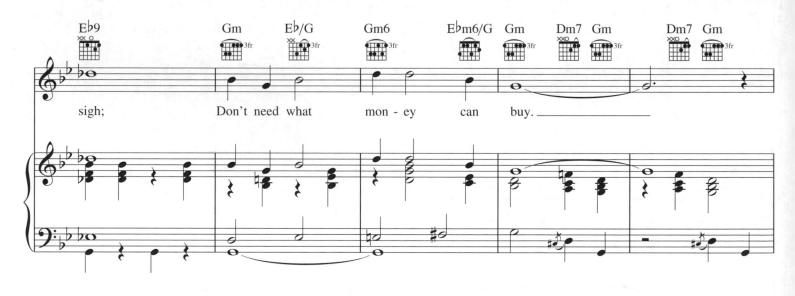

I'VE GROWN ACCUSTOMED TO HER FACE

from MY FAIR LADY

Words by ALAN JAY LERNER
Music by FREDERICK LOEWE

IF I LOVED YOU

from CAROUSEL

Lyrics by OSCAR HAMMERSTEIN II
Music by RICHARD RODGERS

IF I WERE A BELL
from GUYS AND DOLLS

By FRANK LOESSER

JUST IN TIME

from BELLS ARE RINGING

Words by BETTY COMDEN and ADOLPH GREEN
Music by JULE STYNE

IF I WERE A RICH MAN

from the Musical FIDDLER ON THE ROOF

Words by SHELDON HARNICK
Music by JERRY BOCK

Fm   F#dim7   G7   C7

one more lead - ing no - where just for show.   I'd fill my

rall.

F   G7   C   A7

yard with chicks and tur - keys and geese and ducks for the town to see and hear;

Dm7   G7   C   C7

squawk - ing just as nois - i - ly as they can.   And each loud

Fm   Bb7   Ebmaj7   Gm7b5   C7

quack and cluck and gob - ble and honk will land like a trum-pet on the ear;   as

(imitate sounds)

if to say here lives a wealth-y man._____ (Sigh)

man. I see my wife, my Gold - e, look-ing like a rich man's

wife with a prop-er dou-ble chin, su-per-vis-ing meals to her heart's de-

light. I see her put-ting on airs and strut-ting like a pea-cock.

THE IMPOSSIBLE DREAM

(The Quest)

from MAN OF LA MANCHA

Lyric by JOE DARION
Music by MITCH LEIGH

THE LADY IS A TRAMP

from BABES IN ARMS

Words by LORENZ HART
Music by RICHARD RODGERS

THE LAST NIGHT OF THE WORLD

from MISS SAIGON

Music by CLAUDE-MICHEL SCHÖNBERG
Lyrics by RICHARD MALTBY, JR. and ALAIN BOUBLIL
Adapted from original French Lyrics by ALAIN BOUBLIL

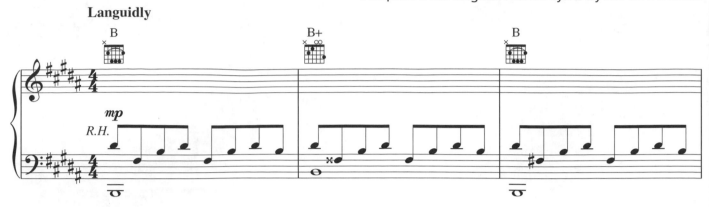

CHRIS: In a place that won't let us feel, ___

in a life where noth-ing seems real ___ I have found you, ___

LUCK BE A LADY
from GUYS AND DOLLS

By FRANK LOESSER

yet be-fore this eve-ning is o-ver, you might give me the brush. ___ You

might for-get your man-ners, you might re-fuse to stay, and so the best that I can do is

Brightly, in 2

pray. _____

Luck be a la-dy to-night. _____

LULLABY OF BROADWAY

from 42ND STREET

Words by AL DUBIN
Music by HARRY WARREN

MACK THE KNIFE
from THE THREEPENNY OPERA

English Words by MARC BLITZSTEIN
Original German Words by BERT BRECHT
Music by KURT WEILL

side - walk ____ Sun - day morn - ing ____ lies a
Mil - ler ____ dis - ap - peared, dear, ____ af - ter

bod - y ____ ooz - ing life; ____ some - one's
draw - ing ____ out his cash; ____ and Mac -

sneak - ing ____ 'round the cor - ner. ____ Is the
heath spends ____ like a sail - or. ____ Did our

some - one ____ Mack the Knife? ____ From a
boy do ____ some - thing rash? ____ Su - key

MAKE SOMEONE HAPPY

from DO RE MI

Words by BETTY COMDEN and ADOLPH GREEN
Music by JULE STYNE

MAME
from MAME

Music and Lyric by
JERRY HERMAN

With a lilt

You coax the blues right out ___ of the horn, Mame, ___
You've brought the cake-walk back ___ in-to style, Mame, ___

you charm the husk right off ___ of the corn, Mame. ___
you make the weep-in' wil-low tree smile, Mame. ___

You've got the ban-joes strum-min' and plunk-in' out a tune to beat the
Your skin is Dix-ie sat-in, there's reb-el in your man-ner and your

MAMMA MIA
from MAMMA MIA!

Words and Music by BENNY ANDERSSON,
BJÖRN ULVAEUS and STIG ANDERSON

MATCHMAKER

from the Musical FIDDLER ON THE ROOF

Words by SHELDON HARNICK
Music by JERRY BOCK

Tempo di Valse

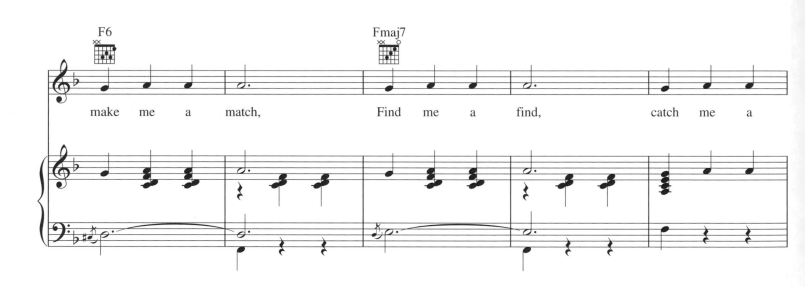

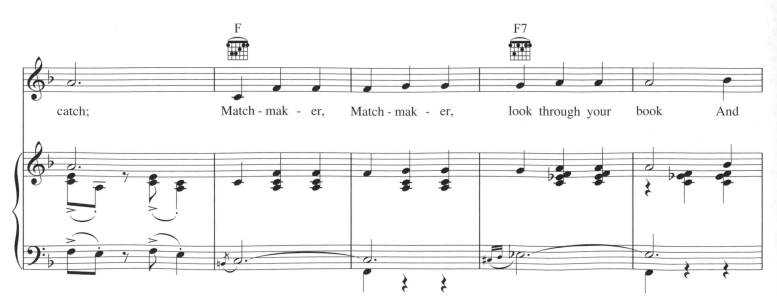

CODA

not that I'm sen - ti - men - tal. It's

just that I'm ter - ri - fied.

Match - mak - er, Match - mak - er, plan me no plans, I'm in no

rush, May - be I've learned Play - ing with match - es a

MEMORY
from CATS

Music by ANDREW LLOYD WEBBER
Text by TREVOR NUNN after T.S. ELIOT

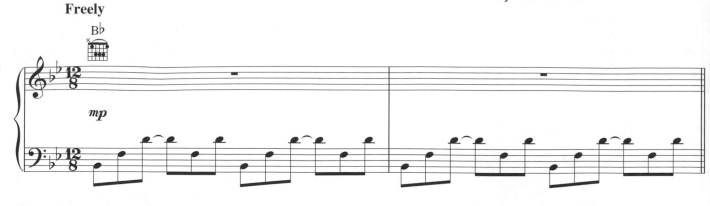

Mid - night. _____ Not a sound from the pave - ment. _____ Has the moon lost her
Mem - ory _____ all a - lone in the moon - light _____ I can smile at the

mem - ory? _____ She is smil - ing a - lone. _____ In the
old days, _____ I was beau - ti - ful then. _____ I re -

Burnt out ends of smo - ky days, ___ the stale cold smell ___ of

MY FUNNY VALENTINE
from BABES IN ARMS

Words by LORENZ HART
Music by RICHARD RODGERS

THE MUSIC OF THE NIGHT
from THE PHANTOM OF THE OPERA

Music by ANDREW LLOYD WEBBER
Lyrics by CHARLES HART
Additional Lyrics by RICHARD STILGOE

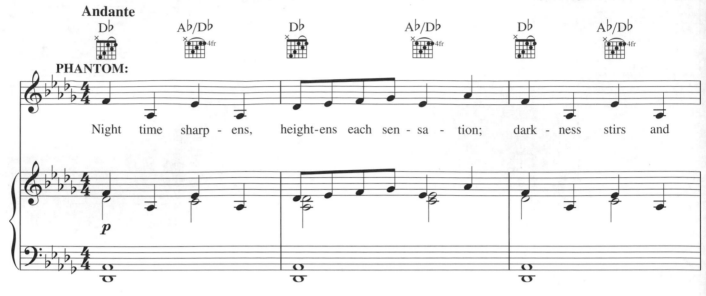

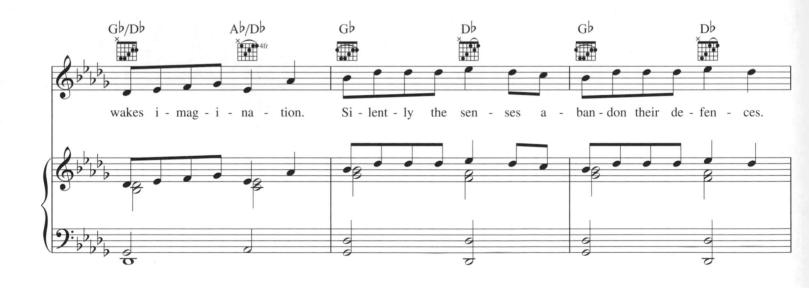

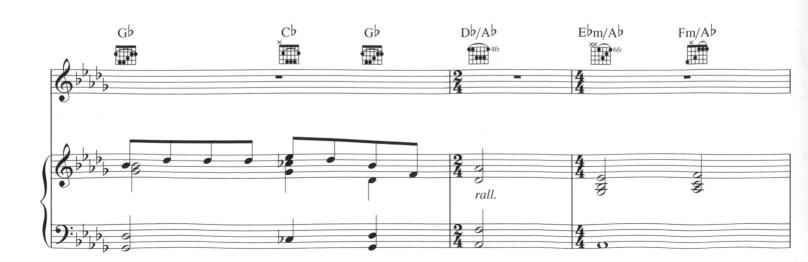

Float - ing, fall - ing, sweet in - tox - i - ca - tion. Touch me, trust me,

sa - vour each sen - sa - tion. Let the dream be - gin, let your dark - er side give in to the

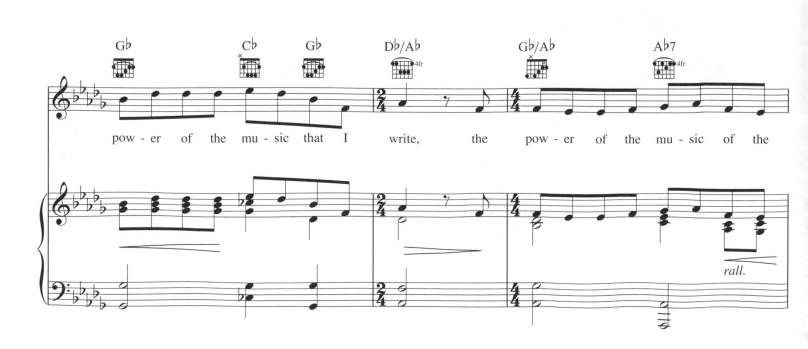

pow - er of the mu - sic that I write, the pow - er of the mu - sic of the

MY FAVORITE THINGS

from THE SOUND OF MUSIC

Lyrics by OSCAR HAMMERSTEIN II
Music by RICHARD RODGERS

MY HEART STOOD STILL

from A CONNECTICUT YANKEE

Words by LORENZ HART
Music by RICHARD RODGERS

OH, WHAT A BEAUTIFUL MORNIN'

from OKLAHOMA!

Lyrics by OSCAR HAMMERSTEIN II
Music by RICHARD RODGERS

OL' MAN RIVER

from SHOW BOAT

Lyrics by OSCAR HAMMERSTEIN II
Music by JEROME KERN

OKLAHOMA
from OKLAHOMA!

Lyrics by OSCAR HAMMERSTEIN II
Music by RICHARD RODGERS

OLD DEVIL MOON

from FINIAN'S RAINBOW

Words by E.Y. "YIP" HARBURG
Music by BURTON LANE

ON MY OWN

from LES MISÉRABLES

Music by CLAUDE-MICHEL SCHÖNBERG
Lyrics by ALAIN BOUBLIL, JEAN-MARC NATEL,
HERBERT KRETZMER, JOHN CAIRD
and TREVOR NUNN

ON A CLEAR DAY
(You Can See Forever)
from ON A CLEAR DAY YOU CAN SEE FOREVER

Words by ALAN JAY LERNER
Music by BURTON LANE

ON THE STREET WHERE YOU LIVE

from MY FAIR LADY

Words by ALAN JAY LERNER
Music by FREDERICK LOEWE

ONE
from A CHORUS LINE

Music by MARVIN HAMLISCH
Lyrics by EDWARD KLEBAN

PEOPLE
from FUNNY GIRL

Words by BOB MERRILL
Music by JULE STYNE

PEOPLE WILL SAY WE'RE IN LOVE

from OKLAHOMA!

Lyrics by OSCAR HAMMERSTEIN II
Music by RICHARD RODGERS

Sweet - heart they're sus - pect - ing things.
They'll see it's al - right with me.

Peo - ple will say we're in love.
Peo - ple will say we're in

love.

POPULAR
from the Broadway Musical WICKED

Music and Lyrics by
STEPHEN SCHWARTZ

A tempo
Dm G Gm7 B♭ Csus C
ly You're gon-na grin and bear it your new-found pop-u-lar-it -
f
F N.C. F C B♭(add9) F
y La la la la
8va
Gm7 B♭ Gm7 B♭ Csus
You'll be pop-u-lar Just not quite as pop-u-lar
(8va)
loco
C F C B♭(add9) C F
as me!

PUT ON A HAPPY FACE

from BYE BYE BIRDIE

Lyric by LEE ADAMS
Music by CHARLES STROUSE

SEASONS OF LOVE

from RENT

Words and Music by
JONATHAN LARSON

'S WONDERFUL

from FUNNY FACE

Music and Lyrics by GEORGE GERSHWIN
and IRA GERSHWIN

Moderately

Life has just be - gun.   Jack has found his   Jill.
Don't mind tell - ing you,   in my hum - ble   fash,

Don't know what you've   done,   but I'm all a -   thrill.
that you thrill me   through,   with a ten - der   pash.

How can words ex - press   your di - vine ap -   peal?
When you said you   care,   'mag - ine my e -   mosh.

SEND IN THE CLOWNS
from the Musical A LITTLE NIGHT MUSIC

Words and Music by
STEPHEN SONDHEIM

SMOKE GETS IN YOUR EYES

from ROBERTA

Words by OTTO HARBACH
Music by JEROME KERN

Yet to-day___ my love has flown a-way;___ I am with - out my

love. Now laugh-ing friends de - ride tears I can-not

hide,_____ so I smile and say, "When a love-ly flame

dies, smoke gets in your eyes."_____

SEPTEMBER SONG
from the Musical Play KNICKERBOCKER HOLIDAY

Words by MAXWELL ANDERSON
Music by KURT WEILL

SEVENTY SIX TROMBONES

from Meredith Willson's THE MUSIC MAN

By MEREDITH WILLSON

March tempo

Sev - en - ty

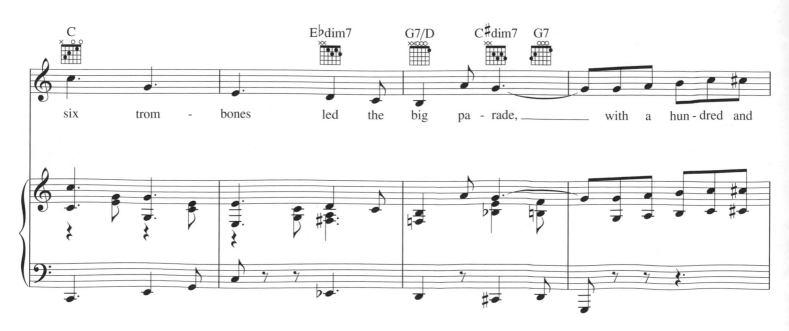

six trom - bones led the big pa - rade, _____ with a hun - dred and

SHE LOVES ME

from SHE LOVES ME

Words by SHELDON HARNICK
Music by JERRY BOCK

SOME ENCHANTED EVENING

from SOUTH PACIFIC

Lyrics by OSCAR HAMMERSTEIN II
Music by RICHARD RODGERS

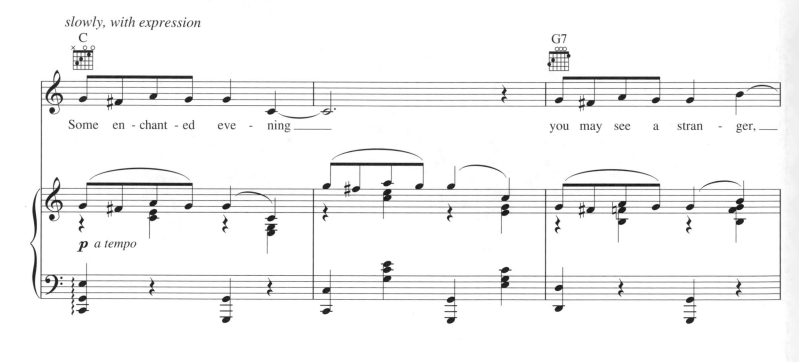

Some en-chant-ed eve-ning ____ you may see a stran-ger, ____

____ you may see a stran-ger ____ a-cross a

SOMEWHERE

from WEST SIDE STORY

Lyrics by STEPHEN SONDHEIM
Music by LEONARD BERNSTEIN

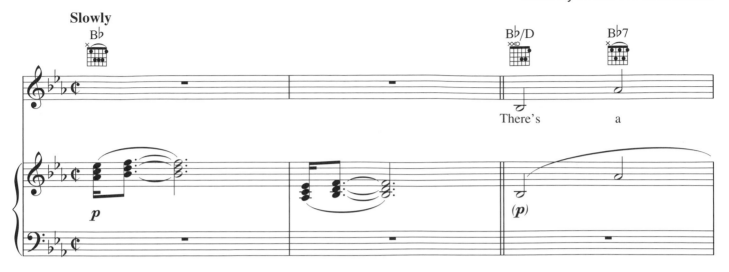

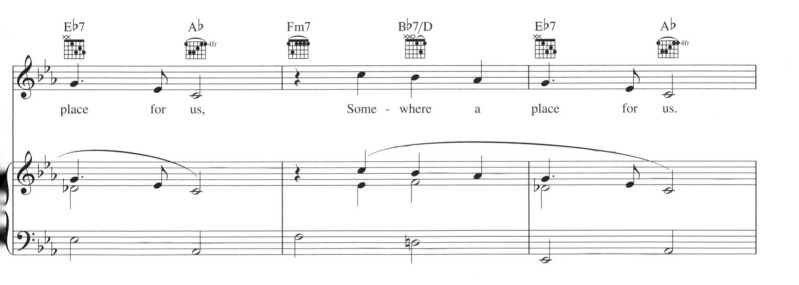

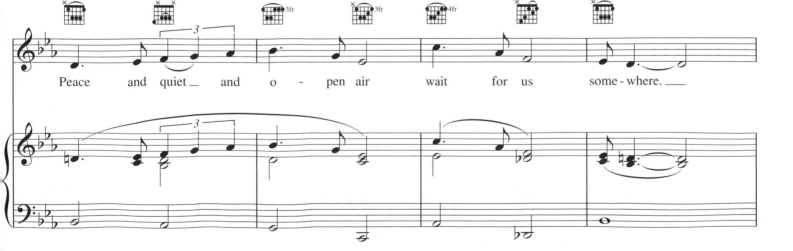

THE SOUND OF MUSIC
from THE SOUND OF MUSIC

Lyrics by OSCAR HAMMERSTEIN II
Music by RICHARD RODGERS

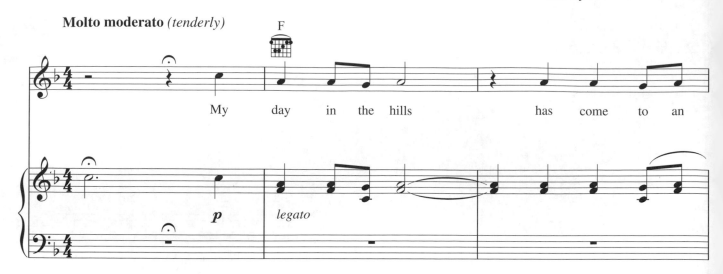

Molto moderato *(tenderly)*

My day in the hills has come to an

end, I know. A star has come out to tell me it's

time to go. But deep in the dark green shad - ows are

STRIKE UP THE BAND

from STRIKE UP THE BAND

Music and Lyrics by GEORGE GERSHWIN
and IRA GERSHWIN

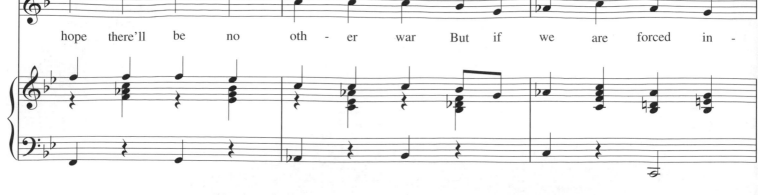

hope there'll be no oth - er war But if we are forced in -

to one The flag that we'll be fight - ing for, Is the

Red and White and Blue one! We do not fa - vor war a - larms

molto marcato

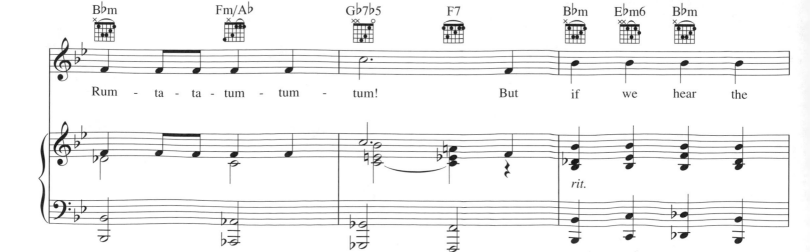

Rum - ta - ta - tum - tum - tum! But if we hear the

rit.

SUNRISE, SUNSET
from the Musical FIDDLER ON THE ROOF

Words by SHELDON HARNICK
Music by JERRY BOCK

THE SURREY WITH THE FRINGE ON TOP

from OKLAHOMA!

Lyrics by OSCAR HAMMERSTEIN II
Music by RICHARD RODGERS

When I take you out to-night with me, _____

Hon - ey, here's the way it's goin' to be: _____

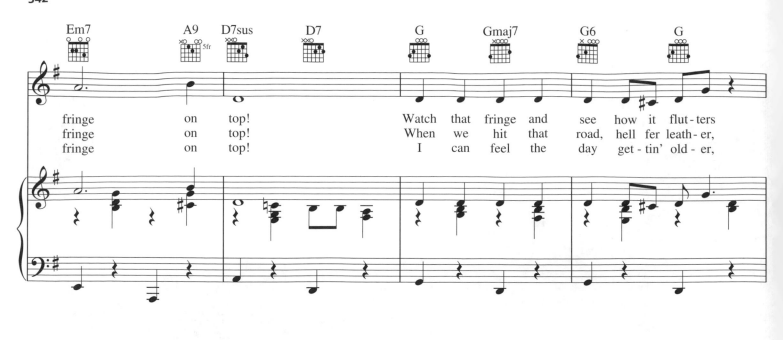

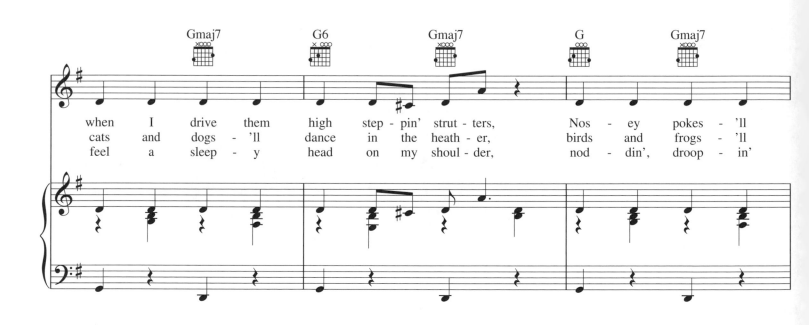

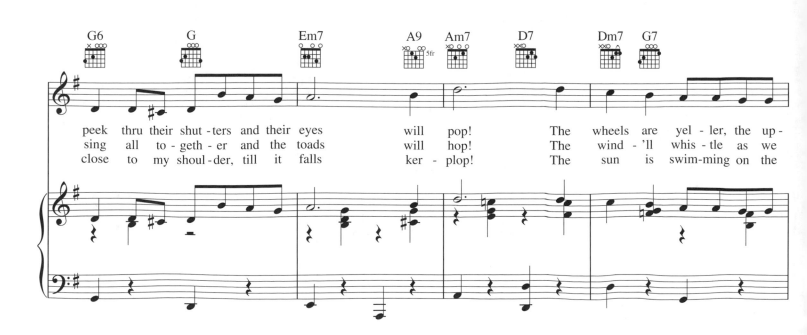

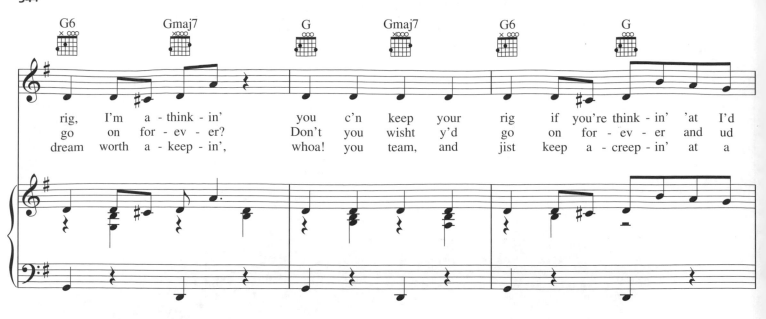

rig, I'm a-think-in' / you c'n keep your rig if you're think-in' 'at I'd
go on for-ev-er? / Don't you wisht y'd go on for-ev-er and ud
dream worth a-keep-in', / whoa! you team, and jist keep a-creep-in' at a

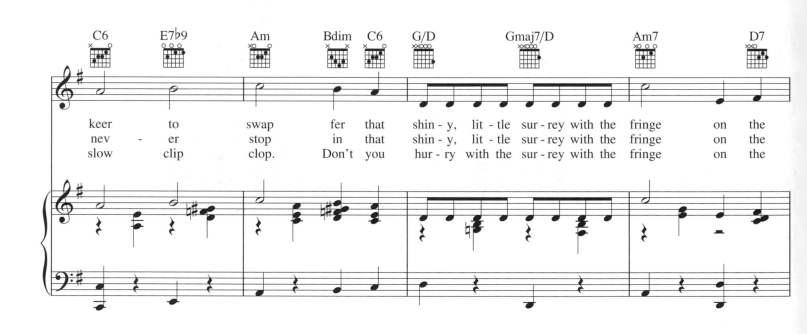

keer to swap fer that shin-y, lit-tle sur-rey with the fringe on the
nev-er stop in that shin-y, lit-tle sur-rey with the fringe on the
slow clip clop. Don't you hur-ry with the sur-rey with the fringe on the

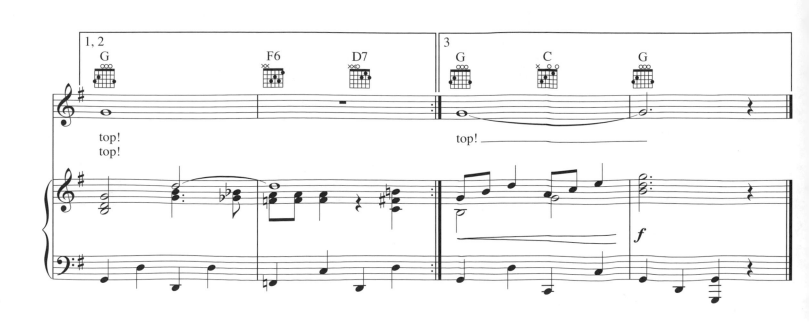

top!
top!

top!

TILL THERE WAS YOU

from Meredith Willson's THE MUSIC MAN

By MEREDITH WILLSON

THERE'S NO BUSINESS LIKE SHOW BUSINESS

from the Stage Production ANNIE GET YOUR GUN

Words and Music by
IRVING BERLIN

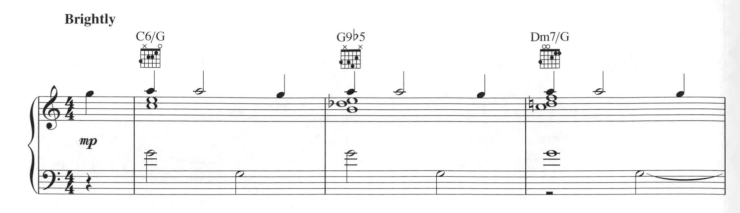

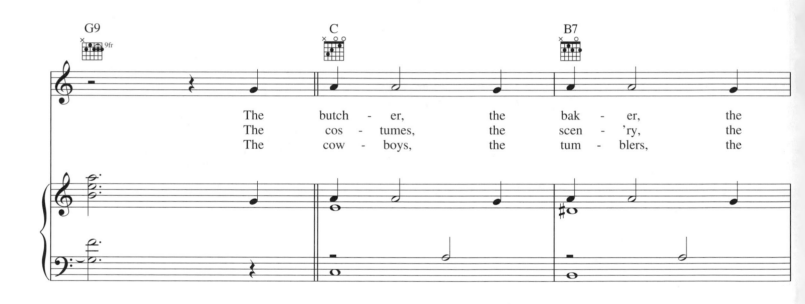

The butch - er,   the bak - er,   the
The cos - tumes,   the scen - 'ry,   the
The cow - boys,   the tum - blers,   the

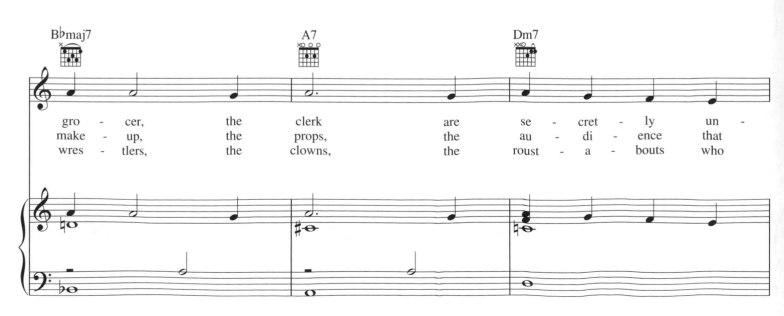

gro - cer,   the clerk   are se - cret - ly un -
make - up,   the props,   the au - di - ence that
wres - tlers,   the clowns,   the roust - a - bouts who

C6

show   peo - ple. They   smile   when ___
show   peo - ple. They   don't   run ___
show   peo - ple. They   smile   when ___

C7

C7/G   **Fmaj7**   **F6**

___ they   are   low. _____
___ out   of   dough. _____
___ they   are   low. _____

Dm7   **Bb7b5**

E - ven   with   a   tur - key   that   you   know   will   fold. ___
An - gels come   from   ev - 'ry - where with   lots   of   jack. ___
Yes - ter - day   they   told   you   you   would   not   go   far. ___

A7   **Ab7b5**   **G7**

___   You   may   be   strand - ed   out
___   And   when   you   lose ___   it,   there's
___   That   night   you   o - pen   and

THIS NEARLY WAS MINE

from SOUTH PACIFIC

Lyrics by OSCAR HAMMERSTEIN II
Music by RICHARD RODGERS

TOMORROW
from the Musical Production ANNIE

Lyric by MARTIN CHARNIN
Music by CHARLES STROUSE

Moderately slow

The sun-'ll come out _____ to-mor-row, bet your bot-tom dol-lar that to-mor-row _____ there'll be sun! Jus' think-ing a-bout _____ to-mor-row

TONIGHT
from WEST SIDE STORY

Lyrics by STEPHEN SONDHEIM
Music by LEONARD BERNSTEIN

The complete number, "Balcony Scene," is a duet for Maria and Tony, adapted here as a solo.

TRY TO REMEMBER

from THE FANTASTICKS

Words by TOM JONES
Music by HARVEY SCHMIDT

Try to re-mem-ber the
Try to re-mem-ber when
Deep in De-cem-ber, it's

kind of Sep-tem-ber when life was slow and
life was so ten-der that no one wept ex-
nice to re-mem-ber, al-though you know ex-

oh, so mel-low.___ Try to re-mem-ber the
cept the wil-low.___ Try to re-mem-ber when
snow will fol-low.___ Deep in De-cem-ber, it's

UNEXPECTED SONG
from SONG & DANCE

Music by ANDREW LLOYD WEBBER
Lyrics by DON BLACK

Gently ($\quad$ = 76)

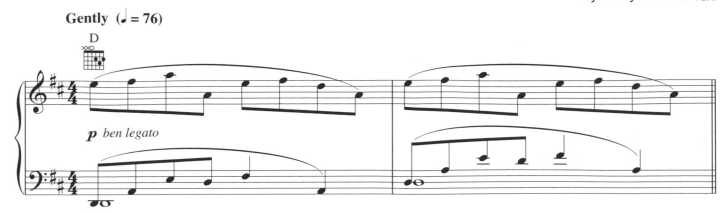

I have nev-er felt like this, for once I'm lost for words, your smile has real-ly
I don't know what's go-ing on, can't work it out at all, what-ev-er made you

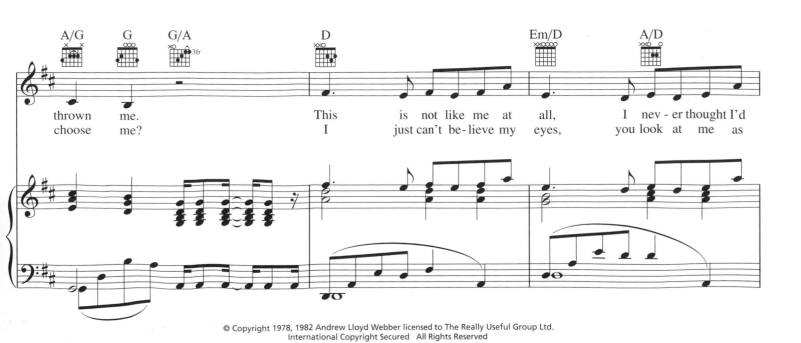

thrown me.
choose me? This is not like me at all, I nev-er thought I'd
I just can't be-lieve my eyes, you look at me as

know the kind of love you've shown me.
though you could-n't bear to lose me.

Now, no mat-ter where I am, no mat-ter what I do, I see your face ap-

pear - ing like an un - ex - pect - ed song, an un - ex - pect - ed

all, I nev-er thought I'd know the kind of love you've shown me.

Now, no mat-ter where I am, no mat-ter what I do, I see your face ap-

pear-ing like an un-ex-pect-ed song, an un-ex-pect-ed

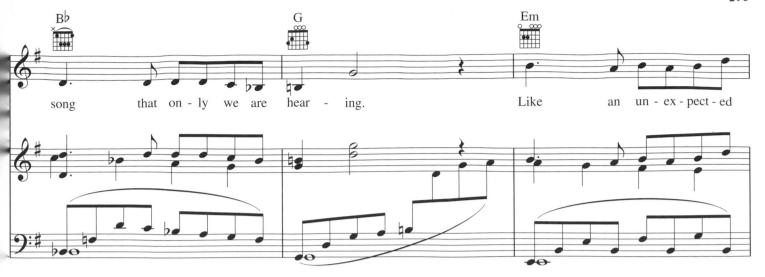

song that on-ly we are hear - ing. Like an un-ex-pect-ed

song, an un-ex-pect-ed song that on-ly we are hear-ing.

WHAT I DID FOR LOVE
from A CHORUS LINE

Music by MARVIN HAMLISCH
Lyric by EDWARD KLEBAN

Kiss to-day __ good-bye,

__ the sweet-ness and the sor-row. __ Wish me luck, __ the

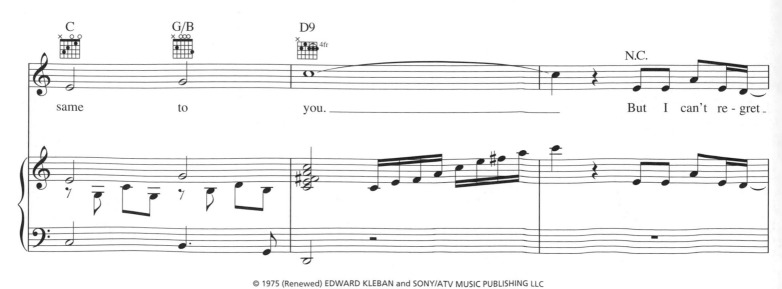

same to you. __ But I can't re-gret __

Dm7♭5 G G/F Em7 G/D Am Am/G
what I did for love. Gone,
Fmaj7 E7sus E7 Am Am/G F♯m7♭5 B7sus B7
love is nev - er gone. As we trav - el
4fr
2fr
E(add2) E G/A A7 Dm7♭5 G7sus/D
on, love's what we'll re - mem - ber.
3fr
G7 N.C. C(add9) C A7sus A7
Kiss to - day good - bye, and point me t'ward to -

WHAT KIND OF FOOL AM I?

from the Musical Production STOP THE WORLD—I WANT TO GET OFF

Words and Music by LESLIE BRICUSSE
and ANTHONY NEWLEY

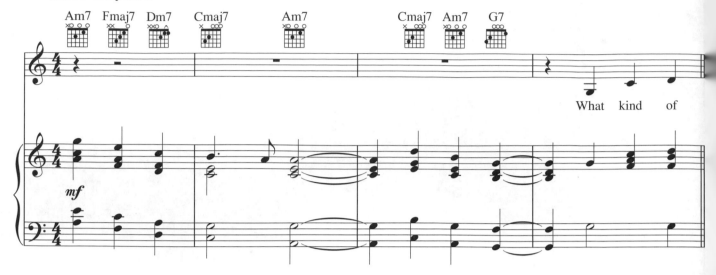

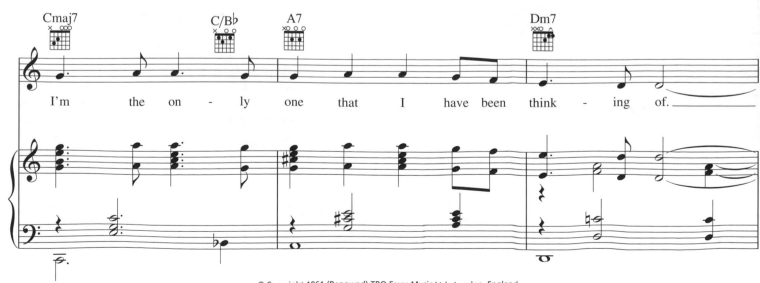

WHERE IS LOVE?

from the Broadway Musical OLIVER!

Words and Music by
LIONEL BART

384

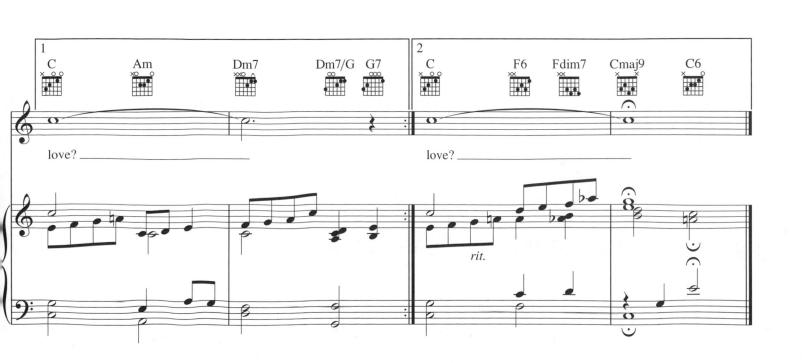

WHO CAN I TURN TO
(When Nobody Needs Me)
from THE ROAR OF THE GREASEPAINT—THE SMELL OF THE CROWD

Words and Music by LESLIE BRICUSSE
and ANTHONY NEWLEY

Slowly, with expression

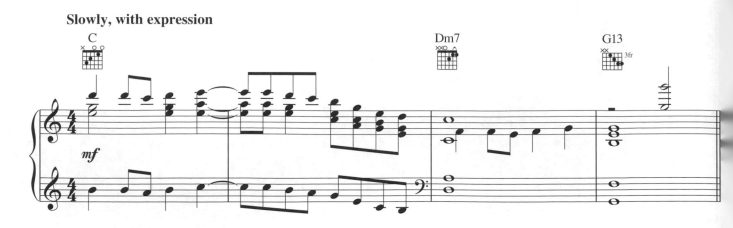

Who can I turn to _____ when no-bod-y needs me? _____ My

heart wants to know and so I must go where des-ti-ny leads me.

WITH ONE LOOK

from SUNSET BOULEVARD

Music by ANDREW LLOYD WEBBER
Lyrics by DON BLACK and CHRISTOPHER HAMPTON,
with contributions by AMY POWERS

YOUNGER THAN SPRINGTIME
from SOUTH PACIFIC

Lyrics by OSCAR HAMMERSTEIN II
Music by RICHARD RODGERS

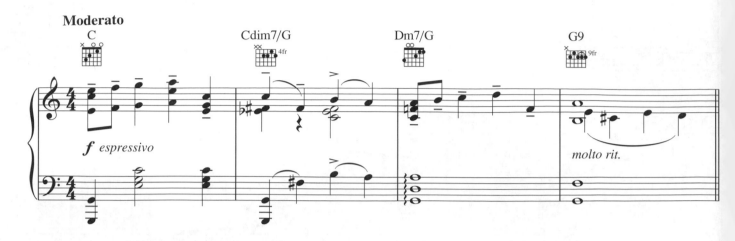

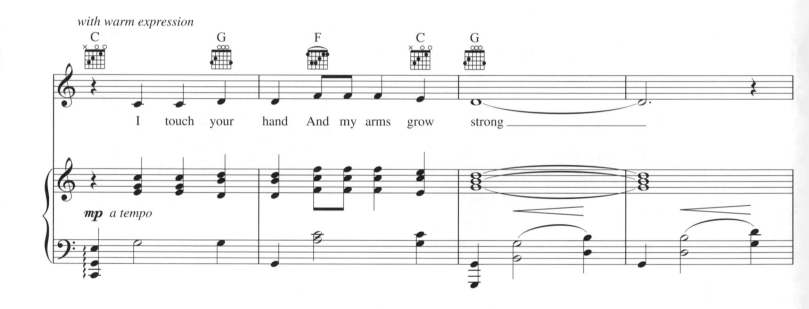

I touch your hand And my arms grow strong

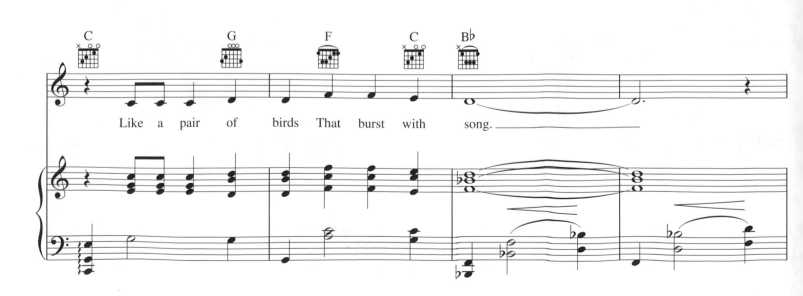

Like a pair of birds That burst with song.

YOU'LL NEVER WALK ALONE

from CAROUSEL

Lyrics by OSCAR HAMMERSTEIN II
Music by RICHARD RODGERS

* alternate lyric: hold your head up high